# The Wonderful World of Dragons

# Coloring Book

20

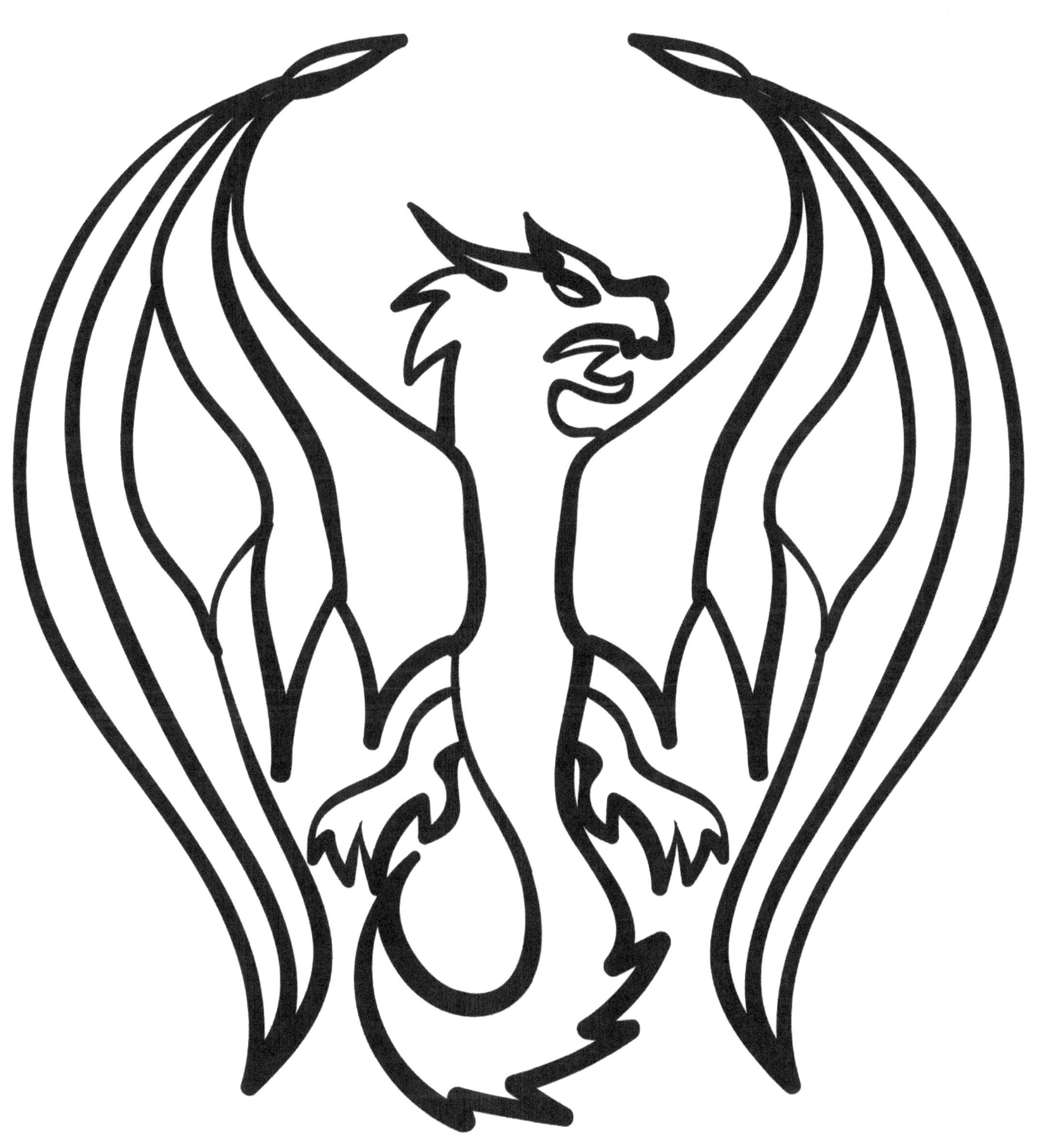

ALWAYS be
YOURSELF
— UNLESS —
you can be a
DRAGON
THEN ALWAYS be a
Dragon

Be on the lookout
for our other
Big Coloring Book
Titles!
Check our author page
on Amazon at:

https://www.amazon.com/Journals-ForYou/e/B08SDWYPJ3